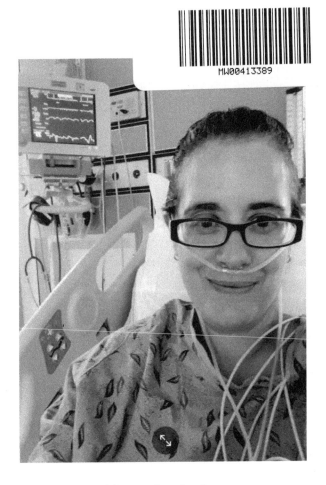

About the Author

Graduated with a Bachelor's Degree in Mass Media
Communication but always had a passion for
Journalism. My love for writing has always been there
and I finally got the opportunity to fulfill my very dream
of making words come to life.

COVID Girl

Andrea Latimer

COVID Girl

Olympia Publishers
London

www.olympiapublishers.com
OLYMPIA PAPERBACK EDITION

A CIP catalogue record for this title is
available from the British Library.

ISBN: 978-1-80074-463-9

First Published in 2022

Olympia Publishers
Tallis House
2 Tallis Street
London
EC4Y 0AB
Printed in Great Britain

Dedication

I dedicate this book to my loving mother, Lisa Anne Guastella. Thank you for always inspiring me and pushing me. Your light is seen by so many and I want to recognize the beautiful soul that you are.

Chapter 1

I don't really know where to begin with this as I always wanted to write. Would I have thought I would be writing this? Not in a long shot. I always thought it would be some awesome romance story with this amazing ending. I am not saying this ending isn't going to be awesome. I guess in reality I am just glad the ending didn't happen yet. I decided to sit down and write because not only is everything different, but I was someone that experienced the very thing so many people are scared of. It's that unknown thing that is out there we never expected and at times never even thought could be real. I guess it sure turned out to be real and the aftermath of it was worse than the actual virus. The virus itself isn't what is so scary it is how people react to it and the fear that drives the insane hate and crazy reactions from the human race. See I would think something like this would bring people together to fight, but instead it seemed to divide people. The blame and the backwards steps to blame is almost a killer, just like the virus itself. I guess I always wanted to do a thesis, looking at two sides in a research puzzle and explain my side. Maybe this is just that, just with a twist. Something just tells me to say something as I know this shall pass just as everything does. But the reality is the world has changed our everyday things we so loved to enjoy has just vanished, almost as if our usual life was just a dream, and the actual life we are in, is somewhat of a nightmare. Some say that it is the year 2020, but in reality, it isn't the year, it is just the very circumstances that enfolded for all of us that were unexpected, in a way irreversible. The loss of control is real! It was like one day we all woke up and it was different. You can't enjoy the life you once lived. That very life is gone and is replaced with face masks and outside dining. The question you ask yourself, is this even really real? I actually asked myself this and is now why I am writing this. This isn't supposed to be a best seller with raving reviews, that is not why I am writing this. I am writing this because my reality was flipped upside down like everyone else and I am still alive to write about it. I went on the news to tell my story but that only got me in trouble. I lost people I thought I was close to. I also received these terrible looks and connotations of you are the "Covid Girl". And let's get this straight, heck yes, I was that "Covid Girl", I guess I finally accept it. I am saying it wasn't easy at first, it was like I had AIDS and people wanted to stay so far away from me in the fear of catching such a dramatic, ever-changing disease. I look back now and I am glad I can say I went through it and I never once tried to understand the layer so many do of how I got it of "oh my, who gave it to me?" Because in reality it never mattered, it is a silent mechanism that transmits from one to another. We as humans only had one way not to get this and it was to stay away from other humans. If you ask yourself this, is it so much harder than we actually think? We miss the hugs the kisses and the sensual movements we long for. When this unknown virus arrived, we got told stay away, keep your distance. The problem with that is that we all thrive and long for those very touches. The simple kiss on the cheek from a relative or friend we haven't seen in a while. Suddenly everything we loved and wanted we couldn't control and the little we got from our leaders the government was to stay away. In reality, they couldn't give us more information than that. They couldn't really tell us why we needed the face masks as much as we did. They couldn't tell us why and how this deadly virus really transmitted. All they could tell us was to stay away! That is like telling a bee to stay away from a flower. See it doesn't work that easily because as humans we want to be near each other. We long for those hugs and those embraces from others.

"Touch is far more essential than our other senses. It is ten times stronger than verbal or emotional contact." Saul Schanberg in A Natural History of Senses.

This is so true as I remember in the beginning when the government officials said to shut down. I asked myself, what in the world does that really mean? They first shut down sporting events and things with large gatherings. I thought to myself, all right I can deal with that. I mean I can do without seeing a baseball game for some time, no big deal. Oh, and a football game all right cool. The news didn't end there, but that is where it began the whole social distancing from everything you thought you loved and enjoyed, that soon would be gone, wiped away like a bug on a windshield when the wiper hits it. It just smeared everything all over that windshield and none of us had one way to change it. That very windshield would end up being me later, but let's not get ahead of ourselves.

So, as things starting changing its like your mind played a game with itself, like it's all right, not too bad. Then it was like boom, everything shut down, no more trips to a restaurant to have a steak dinner with friends, or no trip to the beach of Hawaii that you and your family had planned for over a year. It was like standing there wondering, can this really be real? I asked myself this several times throughout many months. Each and every time I thought about it, for some reason it didn't seem real. It was like that dream you just woke up from and it was over and you went about your daily life. For some reason this wasn't what happened. It was like the dream kept going and so did the news of closures and self-isolation. This was hard for everyone, not just on the single people with no one, but even families of four stuck in one home for weeks on end, with no outside environment available. I can tell you from my perspective it was like hell! I wanted so much to just hug a friend or even a client I so enjoyed. I just wanted that human touch and that feeling of closeness. I learned we need that very sense of the outside world. Like that everyday work life that most of us say we can't stand. Try isolation for a month and that work environment looks just amazing. Like I would take that over isolation any day! It was almost as if the world changed directions in the atmosphere and put us upside down. That very feeling I will never be able to really explain other than it was just insane and felt like the craziest thing I ever felt in my life.

All the sudden we were fighting over toilet paper and hand sanitizer. We couldn't see our friends and that is where that true isolation came in. But I guess I should count myself lucky as at least I had toilet paper. I mean these are the things that really crossed my mind. It's okay, I can't see my family but I have toilet paper and hand sanitizer. So, I am good, right? I can survive on this? I mean I was a little more of a survivalist than that. I did buy a crap load of canned goods and let's not mention the Top Ramen I bought in cases. I may or may not have gone and bought more firearms, as I mean let's be real, I thought the world may be ending and I wasn't going out without a fight. I had to make sure I had that toilet paper and those guns to protect my family. I seriously thought of all these things and I bet almost everybody did. It was like you had to decide what was the most important, just like if you were in a fire evacuation, what would you take and what is the most important. This is probably one of the weirdest experiences in your life when it happens. I am sure some people have already had this experience but when it came to us in an instant across the country, I don't think a lot of us really knew how to process what was actually happening. I mean I certainly didn't, I was just some normal person living somewhat of a normal existence. I didn't have to think that far in advance, it was like I lived day by day and that was just all right, there was nothing pressing me to look two to three months into the future, until this came and made me think of what I may need to survive. I probably sounded like a lunatic to my family and friends when I look back. I thought for sure we would be running out of food and this very virus would take down everything. It did, but in a different way than I thought at first. It really wasn't about things we needed to survive it was more the loss that isn't tangible. That hug from your mom you couldn't give or that kiss to your loved one if they got sick. Those were the things you really lost and no money or hoarding could have changed that. I realize that now, as I look back on all the things I thought I could control, like the food, the toilet paper and the hand sanitizer. We all just needed to control something as we couldn't control the real feeling which was missing, the very things that keep us going on a daily basis. It wasn't any of those things it was those touches and embraces. As humans though we tend to try and grasp what we can control.

"Circumstances are beyond human control, but our conduct is in our power." Benjamin Disraeli

I tried so hard at that time to grasp the new reality and control what I could but I guess I just wished I could make it better and that it would eventually go away. The very virus that came would disappear and all the problems would go away. I would be able to control these few things to create the same world I once lived in. In reality it all fell apart, no matter how much control I thought I had. No matter how hard I tried the pieces fell around me, but I still had that toilet paper.

Chapter 2

That control followed weeks later as things started slipping away more and more. The news briefings made everything a little worse. Like the thoughts of things being normal changed to never being normal again. It's weird when you realize things won't be the same. You start to rationalize to yourself that everything will be fine and things will be all right. But in reality, it won't, at least for the time being. I remember sitting there and thinking all right, things will eventually be better. Right? They had to be, it was just a small time and it would pass very soon. That very thought would stick in my mind for months to come but the fact was it never really passed soon. The reality I didn't want to believe was my actual reality and it wouldn't be going away. I kept thinking it would but as those months passed it made itself clear that Covid-19 would be around not just for a short time but a window that no one could have predicted.

As the government started to mandate stay at home orders and businesses across the United States started to close, the reality started to become clearer. I will never forget the last day I sat inside a restaurant. It has now been engrained in my mind. I can remember what I ate and the two people that joined me. The funny part about that is those exact people would never make it on the other side of the fence with me. Had I known that then maybe I would have chosen different people to enjoy my last meal with. Funny how things in life come full circle sometimes, but we will get to that later. I remember the restaurant had made all these new arrangements keeping all tables six feet apart. As you walked in the once cozy place was like a barren desert. There were only a few tables where so many had been just the week before. There was only one other group of people that dared to come out that day. The place was almost silent and the waitress was able to spend some major quality time with us. That part was actually really nice when I think back. As we all finished our entrees the waitress came back and asked us for dessert. We all looked at each other and told the lovely waitress no we are good. Instead of bringing the bill she brought us cookies and milk. I remember us all smiling from ear to ear on how nice the gesture was.

She said, "This is on me!"

We all enjoyed every last crumb of those cookies, when she finally did bring the bill, I left her probably the biggest tip of my life. It was that simple gesture that created so much happiness just for that moment and I thought she deserved the world that day. As we all got up to leave two of us went outside as the other girl went to use the restroom. She later told us the waitress came up to her and just thanked her, that she really needed that as all the hours had been getting cut. That day would mark the last day I ever stepped foot in a restaurant for months. If I had known that I would have ordered every single thing on that menu. That day will always forever stick out to me because the events that occurred after that day would bring me down a totally different unexpected path that I would never have expected.

Chapter 3

The next day started off like any other normal day, but everything would forever change for me that very day. The job I had loved for almost four years was suddenly gone. I went home and drank a little too much and just cried. My life was slowly falling apart around me, one piece at a time. I went online like millions of Americans did that day. I stared at the completed screen with disbelief to what now my new life looked like. I had no job and the world I once had loved was now gone. It was like someone blew the candle out and all that was left was cold wax. I fell into this abyss like state where I didn't want to get out of bed. I mean was there really a reason to? I was that daily gym rat Monday through Friday and that was gone and so was the job. I was left within my thoughts and maybe some very tasty wine bottles. Good thing I stored those so I could enjoy them when I found myself in a broken state, with nothing but those. I can tell you those wine bottles might have gotten me through the next few weeks as my purpose faded into the distance. I tried my best to think positive but I just sort of disappeared from everyone. I mean that was what we were supposed to do. We were told to social distance. That time was not something I would ever like to repeat or I wouldn't recommend it to anyone. A few close friends that again I can't mention, but you know who you are, would call and make me get out of bed. Which is why this human interaction is so important. We need a support system and we need to have people that love and care about us.

"Human interaction is the key force in overcoming resistance and speedy change." Atul Gawande

Boy did I want that change and needed it as I sat alone, with all the purpose I had simply gone. This isn't supposed to be some sad story, that is not why I am telling it, but I am sure so many felt that same way. The loss of total control was so relevant among so many, I have to touch on this. So many people lost everything around them, their lively hood, there intimate connections and their very existence. I think that is why this really was so hard for not only me but others. Things were stripped away we never thought would be. I mean we couldn't even go see a movie or go to a bowling alley. We were all confined to our little homes and were isolated. So many were left isolated without a job or any income coming in. The government then stepped up to help this which I will admit helped me to not go totally insane. That's pretty bad when the one thing you are happy with is the government. I still laugh to this day thinking of just how amazing that was and it truly did help me through. During this time, I was fortunate that another company decided to hire me. I was a bit shocked because I really hadn't put myself out there. Like who would be hiring now? They were like the angels that were sent my way to help me get through this total desperation that I felt. I will always remember their kindness and appreciate that very feeling. As I started to embark on a new career in the midst of a worldwide pandemic, I felt blessed. I was a little bit unsure on what this new job would look like considering all the limitations that were still set in place. I took the leap anyways and gave it the very best I could. I had to, that was the only thing you really could do. Society still seemed to be at total stand still. Still nothing open with no possible date to reopen. Across the country workers started picketing and saying it was their right to work. Governors in each state were allowed to decide their orders. I don't get into politics much but I have to say if people can't feed their family's they should be allowed to make the decision to work. I think this is one of those things that people will always have different views about, but in reality, if you wanted to go to work, I think you should have been allowed to. Granted, yes, the government is trying to protect everyone, but at what cost? You can disagree with me I will look forward to your hate mail. Those crazy things I receive make me at first mad, but then I think feel really sorry for you. Not everyone is going to have the same opinion and that is what America was made of, something called Democracy. I think a lot of people have failed to see other people's perspectives. This is very sad! I have also noticed that people really like to blame each other. I think people need to take responsibility for their own actions, it really isn't always someone else fault. That is my opinion which hey, you can hate me for, that is just all right with me. I personally wouldn't want my children to starve. We need to move on until that hate mail becomes a pile on my desk. I'm sure it is already getting mailed!

Chapter 4

As the new job started things started to slowly open up in the counties around me. This was like the best thing in the world as I had felt like I was a prisoner in my own home for not days but months. The thought of going out into the world again was one of the greatest feelings. I know that sounds a little crazy but it really was one of the best feelings of my life. I was thinking, where is going to be the first place I visit? What am I going to order, let me look at the menu? It was almost like being a kid in a candy store. Life seemed to move on a little bit like a normal reality during this time. Things were still different. There were still the same spaces that were implemented with tables being apart. There were also plastic barriers between your pedicure chairs. But I thought I will take this just to be able to go out in the world again. I missed the very essence of being social! That was my very existence in the world, to be around people and make people happy. I wanted to laugh with my friends and my clients. I wanted to embrace the world I had loved that so suddenly disappeared. I had always been that person that loved being in a crowd and wanted to feel the energy of the people around me. That feeling I wanted back! I started to go out as things opened and as I look back, maybe I shouldn't have, but I wanted to. I don't regret doing the very things that made me happy. I couldn't sit in the house any more by myself. I needed that companionship. I needed to feel alive like I once had. Several people have asked me if I would have done anything different. Sure, I mean we all can do things better or a little different to get a better outcome at times. This though is life and we make decisions that at the time feel very right and make total sense. So, when I look back I would never take the experiences back. I needed every encounter that I had during that time. I needed the lake days with my friends. I needed those lunches with clients. Some could say that is very selfish, but in reality, it was my decision to be out. It was my decision to take the risk every day that I did. It was this invisible virus, so at the time I thought, well, I will be just fine it will be like the flu. I am young enough and am in pretty good shape. I don't smoke cigarettes and I at least do fifty burpees a week. I should be just fine if I get this unseen virus. There is no way this can take me out, I have no pre-existing conditions or something that will make it to where I can't just fight this off. Now, these are the things I wish I could go back in time and realize that I was in fact not invincible and that this virus could have packed more of a punch than I originally thought. I could have been more careful of course but I still wanted to live my life. I guess I saw it this way…

If I leave my home every day and get into a car and drive to work, I have that chance of never making it back home that day. I risk something every day, we all do! Whether we like to see it this way or not every day is a risk we take.

When this virus came, we were all so afraid we didn't want to go out, to drive to work, in the chance we may contract this and never make it to the next day without realizing we actually do this every day of our life. We always take risks that may be out of our control. So, I guess, I looked at it as this was a risk I was willing to take to keep living the life I wanted to live. I still do not regret going out, I guess you can call me a risk taker of life. Really looking forward to the hate mail now. That though is reality, you can view it another way and that is okay with me. We all have our own opinions in life. Mine though was that I take a risk every day to live in this world. I took the chance! You are probably screaming you fool; how could you say that? If I was standing in front of you right now, I would say, yes, this fool wanted to live and take my chance, just like as I have done for the past forty years of my life. So, fool? I would say more of a realist, but you can call me that. I think at this point you can take almost anyone's cruel comments. You get used to it which is sad but at the same time it can humble you. I would never be writing this if everyone was just so nice to me. I wouldn't have taken the time to write it. I am writing it to say that there are things that really need to change in how people treat one another. That's why I am still here, maybe to express this. We all may not agree with the other persons view, but there is a respect that for some reason we have lost as a society. We would rather burn buildings down to get our point across. Why? My opinion, which is only my thoughts, is because we want to be heard but we feel no one is listening. We have to prove a point and the way to do this can be at times to provoke a certain behavior that isn't always kind so it is noticed. That very thing that we are trying to prove was actually lost in the action. Through all of this I would have loved to see people come together to help each other. I saw it divide everything and everyone. Which is so sad as we really could have come together to help one another. Instead, people blamed each other and were cruel to each other. No one expected this to come into our world and turn it upside down within days, but it did. I did everything I could to try and live a normal life. So, I did just that I lived just as I always had. I took clients to lunch, I brought snacks into the offices I always stopped in. I've got very little hesitation and had mostly acceptance when they started opening things. I felt like life was just starting to come back as I once had known it to be. My best friend and I even planned a weekend in Lake Tahoe. This has always been my favorite place in the world ever since I was a kid. It has always drawn me in with its beauty, as if it was a picture you can't ever actually capture. Every time I have ever been there, I have felt at home, like I was supposed to be there. So when we made this plan I was so excited to go. It gave me something to look forward to when everything was just blah. The weeks went on and things seemed as normal as they could. Nothing really crazy was happening other than all the protests across the nation that seemed to take precedence over the actual Covid-19. The issue became something different as huge mobs went through cities and fought over racism and politics. I personally would like to not touch this subject because my hate letters will take over the whole desk, not just a stack. As the world fell apart for a different reason than Covid-19, I was ready to keep living my life. I mean why couldn't I? Wal-Mart was still open, which to this day I will never understand how you can't catch it from there? They closed so many things but left them open throughout the whole epidemic. Again, this is just a question I have always had. I wonder if others asked this? Everything had to close but they got to stay open. This is something to think about if you haven't already. I mean it was really interesting to see what was still open and what was closed. You can still get the illness from anywhere really. My thought behind this is that some of the things we were told about the virus were not actually real. At first facemasks were not required. As the months went on, they required them to walk into any establishment. What is weird is things kept changing. So, as things kept changing, I believed less and less about what I was being told. I didn't really trust the government. I wanted to believe that maybe this whole thing was a farce or some conspiracy theory. None of it could really be real? I could shop at certain stores but others were off limits. It started to feel a bit awkward and unreal. Things really didn't make sense to me and maybe that is what would eventually change my life.

Chapter 5

Tahoe was approaching and right before the trip this crazy man came back into my life and expressed his feelings. I have personally never had a man come back the way he did and tell me he couldn't be without me. I don't know if I really believed him at first because, I mean, people can say anything, right? And boy was I pissed at him; I hadn't talked to him in months. Here he was like so many other times before expressing his love and wanting to make changes. I believed him once again and thought well he was trying and he cared. He actually loved me like those romantic comedies we all watch. Needless to say, he came and swept me off my feet and things started to feel like puzzle pieces were falling into place. I would be able to have the life I wanted moving forward and having the partner I always dreamed of. I had waited a long time for this crazy man. I knew he was my person the day I met him. I don't know if he knew but I did that day. I have always thought maybe it just took him longer to realize the same thing that I had known for months. He came back for me, not on a magical horse but with a promise to share a future together. He provided a plan to our very consistent long-distance relationship. I fought it for a long time and ended it because I needed more at the time and I don't know if he really could have provided me what I needed. I have realized that sometimes people are just not ready for you and can't provide you what you need at the time. We ended things and there he was explaining to me how he needed me and wanted a life with me. I will never forget this as it may have been the nicest thing anyone has ever done for me. I would like to mention his name but there are no names in this book. His words made everything feel right after so many months of just hurt. He will never fully understand his presence and what that meant to me. Most of my life I haven't had very many people fight and want to make things work. I have had a lot of people just give up, and I am not saying I haven't done this either but it sure is nice when someone wants to fight to be in your life. I really feel like that is the one thing I had always missed out on. People just came and went, never wanting to really stick it out when things got tough. But this crazy man came back to show me something I haven't ever felt from anyone in forty years. He gave me hope when he came back. He gave me hope that the love we had was there and that he wanted to keep us and make things work. He gave me a plan for a future that I so inspired to have. We spent a few weekends just enjoying each other and working towards our life together. I remember he was sad that I already had made plans to go to Tahoe with a few girlfriends. He decided to make his plans to go home and see his family when I went on my trip. He came the night before I left to spend time with me and I was to drive him to the airport the following day. My stomach wasn't feeling great that day and I had a little headache. I didn't think much of it, thinking well this girl loves hot sauce, maybe that could be it. I didn't eat much that night because my stomach wasn't feeling that great. We enjoyed our evening together, and in a way, I was sad he was leaving the next day, and I was leaving for Tahoe. I remember waking up and we forgot to set the alarm. We were late to get him to the airport. We both jumped up like a bat out of hell. We scrambled to get everything together including our minds as we ran out of the house. We made it to the airport with a few minutes to spare. (I hate being late, so to me this creates a huge anxiety. Funny as I wasn't even going to be the one that was late. But that didn't matter. Anxiety is a real thing; it doesn't even have to be you just has to involve you. It sucks trust me!)

We get to the airport and I give him the biggest hug and kiss. I wish him off and have that sinking feeling in the pit of my stomach, like I am going to miss him.

Chapter 6

I felt exhausted as I drove away from the airport, as we didn't get much sleep. I still had to pack and get all my things together for my trip. I had one of the girls going to meet me at my house and we were going to drive together. I made it home finally and felt tired. I figured it was the anxiety of making it just minutes to airport with little sleep. I packed my things and got ready to get on the road. As I waited for my driving partner, I relaxed and thought of crazy man. I was so sad he was gone, and in a way, just wanted to stay there with him. He had never realized how much I really enjoyed his time. My friend finally showed up and we packed her things into the truck, and we started our short but beautiful drive. That drive never gets old. I was starving all the sudden, asking if we could stop to eat because I hadn't been that hungry and my stomach had been a little weird. We stopped at this BBQ place and it hit the spot for my hunger. I still wasn't feeling that awesome. My stomach was just not that great. I ate and just thought, well, it will pass, stomach stuff usually does in like forty-eight hours or so. We get to the cabin and the other girls get there shortly after. I was feeling fine, we all had a few drinks and some tacos. More hot sauce, but I didn't have any of that this time. I was still feeling a bit tired but thought it was from not sleeping enough the night before. All the girls went into the spa and we all had a really nice time together. We were drinking and talking girl talk. It was nice just to be around friends, something that was so missed for so many months. I remember going to bed early that night and was looking forward to the beach day the following day. We all woke up, a few of the girls went on a walk and I cooked us breakfast. We had a long day ahead of us and so we needed some good food to hold us over. After breakfast we all got our stuff ready for the lake. We all piled into two cars and went to the lake. It was just perfect that day, the water was a blue teal, and the weather was just beautiful. I can say was one of the best lake days ever. We all enjoyed the day and half of us went back to the cabin first. And the others stayed back to enjoy a boat ride. I went with the first group and found myself having a hard time breathing on the walk back to the car. I usually walk three miles a day and this was a simple half-mile. When I made it back to the vehicle I thought, well that is super weird, why was I so huffing and puffing? We had dinner plans that night and I actually thought of not going as I just felt tired and a little weirded out about my walk back to the car. I went anyways, figured it's just dinner. During dinner is when I really knew something was majorly wrong. I ordered this salmon dish and it had garlic all over it. I couldn't taste it, like nothing at all. I have to say this was the weirdest experience I have ever had in my life. I couldn't taste a thing? This is when I thought this can't be true right? That was the symptom that stood out to me as Covid-19. I didn't even finish my meal, I asked to go home and did just that. I went back and went straight to bed! I woke up in the midnight hours and a few of the girls were concerned with my breathing. I said how maybe I should go to the hospital as I am having some troubles. A few of the girls called the wrong hospital as I didn't have that medical card any more. Note to self, always take out your old medical card. I finally just said, "I will be all right and don't worry, I will take care of it when I get home."

Chapter 7

Day One

I woke up first thing in the morning and left. A few of the girls stayed behind to take care of closing up the cabin. I went home and I bareley could get up the stairs. I said to myself, this will pass, I will be fine, but in reality, I couldn't breathe at this point. I knew I had this dreadful virus. I knew in every ounce of my being I had this. People tried to strong arm me to go get tested, but in reality, I couldn't get out of bed. I couldn't make it to the kitchen and back. I thought each day it would get better, but it just didn't. I had some really great friends who dropped me food at the door. I was able to make it each and every time, but boy was it a struggle. Then two days after making it home I just couldn't get to the door any more. I made it half way and felt like I was going to pass out and went back to bed. This was the moment I thought to myself, you aren't getting better, you are getting worse. You can't even make it to the door and back. You may actually just die. Let me tell you I contemplated this choice. You might think I am crazy, but I did. That decision would ever change my life and to be honest it was the decision to fight. I am telling you that I didn't want to at first, as I just wanted to give up. I knew though if I stayed like I was, I would die. I will always remember hitting the nine and the one and the last one. I was scared. I had never been in a hospital before, other than to see a loved one. I also thought to myself, what if I go and I never come back? I think that was actually the biggest hesitation I had that day. I knew I was dying, but I didn't want to die by myself. That is what people don't see about this, you are one hundred percent by yourself. No family, no friends are allowed into the room you are in. You are a prisoner, like being in an asbestos abatement containment. Most people will never understand what this is like. I think this is worst then the virus itself. So, I was panicked and remember I suffer from anxiety, so that was full throttle for sure. I called on myself because I was by myself. I took the step to get help and I have to say that may have been the hardest step for me because I am proud, and I was going to be all right without any help. One of those really awesome friends I was talking about who brought me food told me at one time to leave the front door open, just in case. You know who you are and thank goodness you told me that as the paramedics had to get in. I will forever thank you for that! The paramedics arrived and that was scary, they put me on this stretcher. I had some black shorts on and a white tank top and I probably looked like utter hell that day. Of course, all of them were cute as can be as I laid there on a stretcher. I call it my expensive limo ride because let's be real, that is what it is. I am about fifteen miles from the hospital and all I was thinking as every mile past is there is another hundred dollars. I still at this time thought they would release me and all this was just crazy. As the ambulance parked next to the hospital my anxiety was through the roof. It is giving me anxiety just writing this. I knew I was sick but I would be all right and why am I even here? They started poking and prodding me, which has always been my biggest fear in life. With all their poking and prodding they gave me the Covid-19 Test. I already knew the result. It took about an hour and it came back positive... No crap! I remember them trying to convince me to put a catheter in. I was hell bet against that one. I told them nope I will get up and go to the bathroom. I made it that one last time but dammit, I did bareley. The nurse said, "You barely made it, your oxygen level is so low."

I said, "I will be just fine don't you worry about me." I have learned a few things in the hospital, you can tell them no and they have to work around it. The day you can't say no though that is when you get into trouble. Good thing that wasn't me at this exact time! I swear that room felt like a jail cell as no one really came in for hours. I laid there wondering, what was happening? Was I going to die? What were they going to do with me? Where was my mom? Not anyone will ever understand the thoughts you would have in a situation like this. The unknown I think was the craziest thing I ever felt in my life. I had never been so scared and trust me it was the weirdest feeling. It was like you knew you were so very sick and you possibly would not make it another day. They isolated me in this very room for hours. Someone came in and said that they would be admitting you shortly. Well, shortly felt like a lifetime. A doctor came in and asked me a series of questions.

"Do you smoke?" I told him I didn't but did like ten years ago. He asked me a few more questions and left. I sat there in my thoughts thinking to myself, wow, what if me smoking years ago could mean something now? What if it will affect me now? All these things crossed my mind and all I could do was lie there; it was like the worst torture in my life. Nobody came in for hours. I just laid there wishing someone would talk to me just for a minute. The minutes passed and I just tried to talk to my family and loved ones and was so worried about that battery dying. I can't tell you how much that battery meant to me! My charger was in my purse and that was so far away. I watched that battery like it was a first-born child. I was just so shocked I was in this place and even more that I was just so sick. I still though felt like I would be just fine. Things will just go away like a usual flu. Then a tall man, I think was bald with blue eyes, came in and said we are ready to take you.

I said, "Where are we going?"

He said, "You will be going to ICU."

That very moment I thought wow, this is really happening, and I am really sick for them to take me there. As he wheeled me through the doors, all of the sudden I was outside and I felt the breeze and fresh air. I wouldn't feel this for the next seven days. I was so scared and he grabbed my hand and said, "We are taking the long way." The wheels hit the asphalt and all I could do was look up and see the stars. I will never forget them that evening, bright as ever. I think I even said to him how I was scared and he grabbed my hand harder and said, "You will be all right, trust me."

I don't know if I did at that moment but I just remember saying to him, "Thank you for showing me the stars, it may be the last time I see them." I remember crying to myself on that trip and I will forever thank that man for taking me the long way. He may have just said that to me not realizing that it meant the world to me. It's weird when you relive something like this, it creates emotion you may not think you could feel again. Or maybe emotion you don't want to feel again. I have to say, when the stars disappeared, I felt so alone and the long hall of lights were not the same. The breeze wasn't there and it was this long sterile hallway. Like I was being taken into an abyss and I never knew if I would ever be out of it. The hallway finally turned into a big room and then the wheels moved me to this room filled with monitors and things I have never seen before. My heart started racing and I felt so strange. There was a young nurse and he took the bed from the nice man that took me on the long detour. I almost didn't want him to go because I would be left there. I felt hopeless and just scared total shitless. Sorry, I swear, I hope that is all right? If not, I am sorry, because that is so me. The young man made me show me my arm and scanned me like I was an animal they had to track. I gave him my wrist without hesitation, because they were going to help me, right?

Then he said, "We are going to have to shoot you in the stomach with a drug to assist you to not get blood clots." I cringed to myself thinking really, this is what it comes down to. I explained to him that my dad had a blood clot, so I got two a day after that. Maybe I shouldn't have said anything, but I had to I guess, because I wanted to live. I haven't always felt that way, there have been times I really didn't want to be on this planet any more. But here I was and I was faced with death itself and I wanted to fight. I had to, because why? That may be the biggest question even now as I write this. I think I had to because there was more for me to do. I wasn't ready yet! I always thought I would be all right with death when I faced it. The reality was I was a huge sissy when it came to it. I will have gone through a whole box of tissues after this segment. You don't realize it until you are faced with it I guess. So, after I got scanned it's like they knew all my medications I have ever taken in my life.

The young man asked me, "Would you like an anxiety pill?"

Well, hell yes, I want an anxiety pill! Can I have two please, all I wanted was to sleep. The machines were so loud I don't think even two would have worked. He brought one to me anyways. I laid in that room after he left and I was alone. There was no noise other than those loud machines. I tried so hard to sleep but I just couldn't I realized I needed these people because I couldn't even get out of the bed. During the night I had to hit the button on the side of the bed to have someone come help me to go to the bathroom. Remember, I couldn't get up, so they brought a bed pan and you will be humbled when this happens, if it ever does to you. At first, I thought I couldn't do it, I wouldn't let them lift me, I did it myself. I never let them, I always did it myself because I had to. I fought to keep this one thing I could control. I wouldn't give up lifting myself up. It took everything I had every time. But I was strong, or I once was. This part was so in your mind. It was your drive to be all right and that if you can keep the struggle to move yourself up, it would just happen because you wanted it to. I did this every time and let me tell you this struggle was real. It was the worst thing just to go to the bathroom. Reliving this I must say this was the hardest part of the whole thing. My first night in the hospital will be something I will never forget for a minute. I didn't sleep a second and I had to let my pride go. I had to let my everything go that day. The funny thing is you would think that I would have anger that I was here in this situation, but I didn't. I just knew this was it for now, if I survived, I would do something that meant something in this world. Those are the very thoughts that I had. I also thought of all the people that were around me for the week or so. I just hoped they were all right. I just wanted to make sure if I died that no one else did. I didn't want anyone to be in this very exact position that I found myself in. I didn't want them to feel how I felt now. I wanted them to be all right and not get this. I wouldn't have wished this on my worst enemy.

Day 2

I woke this morning and felt the same, not better but the same. The highlight of the day was the morning cafeteria call. I got to pick all my food for the next day. I have to say this was amazing, I wish I could get this service at home. Maybe not the food itself, but that service. For some reason this day felt like I would be all right. I didn't feel amazing, but I felt like I was alive. Wild Rose nurse came in and I really liked her, she made me eat is all I remember but I didn't have an appetite at all at this time. I would try a few bites and she would more or less yell at me to eat more. I would look at her with this, "sure I will eat don't you worry about me" look. That again was my stubborn ass that I am. Don't tell me what to do, I will eat a bite or two and then I will do what I would like to do. I liked her, she got my stubbornness pretty good. She was my nurse for most of the day. Remember you only get to see them for certain amount of time until they leave when their shift was over. This was hard as you get used to them and they are the only soul that you see. They always have full PPE on and you can't even really see their faces. These people should be called angels, as that was what they were to me. They were the only people I saw. They made me eat, they held my hand and they bathed me. They were my everything and there was only one of them at a time. Each and every one of them has made an impression on me that I may be able to really express into words. I just hope they read this, because they are the real angels of the world. They helped me at my very worst. She pushed me to eat that day and I wanted nothing to do with it. In my mind I thought I was doing amazing. I mean, I couldn't get out of bed but I was fine breathing and thought I would be getting out of this joint soon.

Day 3

I would like to call this hell day! For some reason I woke up and I was a mess. I was lying in bed and couldn't breathe at all. I was gasping for just the simplest breath.

All the sudden things seemed to change. Wild Rose put the real oxygen on my face and I knew something was just so wrong. They came and drew my blood, like three times in a few hours. My veins were not all there so they took some out of my hands. I was always afraid of people taking my blood and here I was letting them take it out of my hands. I don't remember much of this day as I was so out of it. This was the day they brought in DNR papers to me and came with a few options that I could choose from. I could barely breath and I would have taken everything they had, other than the respirator. No thank you, as if I couldn't breathe on my own, I didn't feel I needed to still be on this planet. Don't judge me everyone gets their own decision that was mine. I still had my Wild Rose and I remember saying to her, "Can you please just give me something to put me to sleep as I can't breathe anymore?"

She said, "No you are too young and you will keep on breathing."

I remember nodding at her and thinking, yes right. I am going to die here alone, with you as my witness. This day was something I will never really be able to fully explain and you would think I would be able to. It was the worst day of my life and I really did think this was my last, or soon to be my last day. Maybe that's why I wanted to forget about this very day! I barley could lift myself up this day and if I could have died, I would have. There was something in me though that said, you can't, you have to fight. I had that crazy man in my mind, I know it was him. I had finally found him after years of being single and he showed up and expressed things that I never thought a man could. I know deep down inside I had to fight to be with him. I had more to do in this world! He cried that day he talked to me because I think he knew I was really sick and I remember saying to him, "Stop it you have to be strong for me." I wasn't ready yet to let everything go and dammit, I wasn't going to let this virus take me out. It was almost like I had to keep going, or else it won. I had no preexisting conditions. I wasn't that old and I hadn't smoked cigarettes in years. That day though, I didn't see the light, I saw me disintegrating and there was nothing I could do about it. I was so weak and maybe my lack of sleep and the no eating had something to do with this, but in reality, it had everything to do with Covid-19. The doctor came in and offered me plasma from another patient that had made it through with antibodies in their blood. They explained this to me and I went with it. I mean what do you have to lose at this point? They gave me this in my IV for about an hour.

Then the doctor came in and offered me a new antiviral drug called, "Remdesivir."

You have to understand when you think you are dying you will try anything. This day was the big, let's try it and see what happens day. I was a mess. I would have done anything this day! I just wanted to be able to breath and I would have done any drug they presented to me. I know all this was just suspect and they don't know if it really works and who knows the side effects? At this point, it is a risk you have to take. I wanted to live, I wanted to see those very stars again. I wanted to see crazy man! I had to get better. I knew this in my heart, even though throughout this day I just wanted to give up and call it a day. I mean I lived forty years and had been blessed and have really enjoyed my life. It was weird though, these nurses and doctors would not let me just go by the way side. I think they may have been the ones fighting harder than me. My next nurse came in for the evening and boy do I wish I could say her name, but again this is the nameless book. I just have to say she was amazing and just made me smile. I felt like total death and this Rockstar showed up and I was like who is this person? We will call her Rockstar! This person made me laugh like I have never laughed before and I was in the worst shape of my life. She came in with just the best energy I have ever felt. She made me forget that I was where I was. I didn't want her to leave and she was my night person, so I never got to spend that much time with her, but there was just this thing about her that me smile. I hope she realizes that evening, my worst day, her energy got me through the evening. Thank you for your smile and I will always remember you as my Rockstar on my worst day ever.

Day 4

I woke up the next day and still was so weak and let me tell you, they don't let you sleep in the hospital. They wake you up like every four hours to check your vitals. Relaxing is almost impossible. It was four in the morning and they said we need to take your chest x-ray. I mumbled and fought this at all costs, as this meant turning over and actually moving. They said it would be quick so I moved and picked myself up the best way I could and they got that awesome shot of my chest. I wish they would have showed me what it looked like, as it took me so much for them to take that very shot. It may have made me feel better to actually see the picture. They finally left and I settled back into the very comfortable hospital bed to try and go back to sleep. The machines were sounding in the background and sounded like faint growls. I decided to take my phone out and put on some nature sounds. I have to say this worked as the soft rain pellets hit and the ocean waves crashed, I fell fast asleep. It was almost as if the sounds put me somewhere else like I was not in this place, I was somewhere far away. Like in a rainforest where I can feel the fresh droplets hit my face and the birds chirping in the background. I wanted to be there where I could feel alive again. Where I really was didn't feel like I was free. I felt trapped in the room, away from everyone and everything I knew. There was no fresh air, there was no calm sounds. I almost had to make them myself to keep my head right, so I didn't go down that dark spiral of helplessness. This was more than the illness itself; this was a strength that comes out of you when you don't really know what else to do. I thought I was dying, so I needed to be here for these angels to help me, but your mind travels with lack of sleep and all the surroundings. Sometimes that machine beeping made me want to go completely insane. I would look at it and say to myself, what is wrong? The blood pressure wouldn't be reading right or my oxygen dropped. This drove me completely insane. I would hit the nurses' button and make them put on all that PPE just to turn it off! Like mute it please!

I finally got back to sleep and just a few hours later

the vampire showed up. That would be the people who come take your blood. I would see them coming and cringe. Remember, I didn't even want to come to the hospital because of this poking. It was like that horror movie you were watching when they are slowly coming your way and you want to run like hell. I think if I could have run, I would have, each and every time they came. I was though stuck in this bed, without enough oxygen to walk away without even the thought of running anywhere. She came and caught me, at least that's how I want to see it. She got her very valued blood that she looked forward to. Glad that was over! Then how do you go back to bed again, so you end up staying awake waiting for this amazing breakfast to arrive.

I had a new day nurse who I have to call, "Happy".

He brought me that breakfast I just looked forward to and it always disappointed. I mean could we had some sugar Cheerios? Maybe some Frosted Flakes? I mean anything would be better. They always had these casserole things so I always chose the cereal and fruit. That was the safe bet, but still disappointing. I will tell you I lost a lot of weight in this process. I almost felt like I was dwindling away. I was so exhausted and starving. All I told Happy was all I want in life is a Happy Meal.

He would always laugh and say, "We will get you one of those." I don't know if I really believed him as I was stuck in this place. I still tried to believe at some point I would get better and leave, possibly getting that happy meal again. Mind you, I haven't had a Happy Meal in years. For some reason that was all I wanted. I tried to watch the television, but it was at the worst angle and when I moved it the thing would always cut out. This day was no different than the rest, my really awesome non-sugar cereal and the terrible TV. You are stuck then with your thoughts. You can't talk to anyone around you and you are confined to this very small space. There is nothing exciting around you and you can't even get up to go use the bathroom. It leaves you with your smart phone, which thank goodness I had. That was my lifeline to everything I loved and cared about. The days just seemed so long and all I kept thinking to myself was let's try and get out of here. I asked Happy what I needed to do.

He said you, "You need to get your oxygen level stable in the 90s."

I thought to myself, I have to try, but I knew I wasn't even ready to walk. They came and put these things around my calves to massage them to make sure my muscles didn't atrophy. I couldn't even believe I was in this place. I couldn't move my muscles and had loved working out and keeping my body in the best shape I could. Here I was trying my best and I couldn't even really move. Those things actually felt good, I wish I could have taken them home to massage my muscles when they were sore. I did ask for them when I left, figured why not, but they told me no. You have to try right? The day went on they came gave me another injection in my stomach later and brought my dinner. It was the most precise timing and planning I may have ever experienced. There were things I liked about this, as you always knew what was happening and that was the control that I could take. The fault of this is that there was nothing in the day that made you feel like euphoric. It was just plain and routine. I think what we want is the feeling of euphoria, not the mundane things we do every day. We like the surprises from loved ones. We want the unexpected! I think if you go through something like this it has to make you realize at least one thing. I think mine was the control. I will never be able or do I want to control everything? It is boring and there is so much more to life. Even though some of the unexpected things have been the scariest things, they have proved to be the best blessings.

I felt like I was doing a little better towards the evening. They asked if I could take out the main oxygen and go back to the little nose ones. I said let's do it! I seemed to hold my oxygen. My Rockstar came back that night with her energy I just loved and it gave me such hope that I would be getting better. I was sad to see Happy go for the day, but excited to see her. She came in and we chatted for a while, which was nice as there was never that much contact. You almost felt bad as they are covered and probably hot as hell in the suits and masks. I enjoyed every interaction that I had as that was the only thing that made me keep going and I looked forward to.

Day 5

I started to feel a little better and decided that I needed to start moving around. They pushed me for sure, as at first, I was hesitant. This day I considered my *push day show* these people you can do it. I had questions to myself. What if I can't get up or what if I can't keep my oxygen level up? This was a daily thought as all I wanted to do was feel better. It is weird to not be able to breath and even weirder to be young and unable to breath. This gives me chills just thinking about how it felt to feel this way.

Imagine taking a big inhale and letting it out, but you can't. Like you inhale but only a little air goes in and you try and exhale that little bit and it is hard. Your body tingles to try and take that very breathe.

That is the only way I really know how to describe it. A new nurse came in and she was unbelievable, her name came to me as Twist as she would braid my hair and make me feel like a human again. I never cared for days how my lack of cleanliness was but when I started to feel just a tad better, this mattered. I asked her, "Can you please help me do something with my terrible hair?" Twist did exactly that and made me feel human again and pretty, something I haven't felt in days. This day was the best feeling I had since I came into this prison like setting. I felt clean and just pretty, with a little of myself back. This whole time I was concerned about all the people that may have been exposed to me. I had been in the ICU for five days, no one had their test results back to know if they were positive or negative. This was torture to feel as you lay there, not knowing and hoping no one could get this same thing you did. I checked in daily from the group of people that I was around to see if anyone had gotten test results back yet. This was one of those things that made it even worse. How were the results taking so long when I got mine automatically? Not one person had test results back, but one of the girls said she had some symptoms and that her ex-husband had tested positive and went to the hospital. Other than that, no one else had said they had any symptoms. Even the crazy man I was with got his test results later that day and he was negative. I couldn't have been happier as he was the closest person I was with. I couldn't believe it in a way, how is that even possible? I still to this day will always question this. If this was so contagious, how did no one get it? I guess you could say I gave it to the one person, but really is that possible when her ex-husband went to the hospital the same time I did? Not only did he have it but he had given it to his son. Slowly but surely that day everyone else came back negative and never got it. It was like a big sigh of relief and I can never explain that feeling as each negative test came out.

Day 6

I woke up to the vampire trying to take my blood. That is what I called them, the people that drew blood that is. I was starting to feel a lot better and maybe I had my old personality back. I told them to get out, no blood today! They obliged and left the room and I finally went back to sleep. I listened to the soft calming music of waterfalls so I could feel like I was somewhere else. I think this may have been the best sleep I had during this whole ordeal.

When I finally woke Twist came in and said, "Today is the day. It's time for you to get up and walk around."

I looked at her like she was seriously crazy. I said, "I don't think I am ready for this."

She said, "Do you want to get out of here?"

Well, hell yes, I wanted out! Who wouldn't? I couldn't see or touch anyone I knew. I was eating the worst food ever and I seriously hated the vampires. She gave me that look. I said, "All right I will get up." The whole time I was thinking, you have to do this. I was scared at the same time as I thought, what if I couldn't? What if I was too weak? I haven't tried to get out of the bed in days. I slowly lifted my legs over the bed rail. I watched that oxygen level like my life was determined by it. I pushed myself slowly off the bed. Twist watched me from the corner of the room. She didn't go to help me, she wanted me to do it on my own. My heart was pounding out of my chest. I took one step and then another, never taking my eyes off the monitor. The oxygen level dropped a little, going to ninety-three then ninety-two. I started to panic with my anxiety but said to myself, you have to continue, it's your only way out. I kept going step by step to the bathroom and then back. I finally got back to the bed holding a ninety, oxygen level. I breathed a big sigh of relief as I plopped down.

Twist looked at me and said, "Great job you made it."

I laid back down and tried to relax as to me at that moment it was like I had just landed on planet Mars. I felt winded, but was so happy that I didn't dip below ninety. She said she would let the doctor know and I may just get to go tomorrow. I looked at her with hopeful eyes and wished that she was right. The rest of the day was pretty uneventful. I looked forward to my very plain meals but I have to say they were my highlight. I looked forward to the possibility I would be going tomorrow.

Day 7

I woke up to the vampire at the door. I said, "Not today no more blood."

She said, "The doctor won't let you leave without it."

I rolled over and let her take her last bite on my arm.

I waited a few hours and never heard from anyone. I wanted to be out so bad, I could feel my feet ready to run out of the place. Every minute seemed like an eternity, like I was waiting at a DMV office.

All the sudden a new nurse came in and she said, "You are ready to go."

I didn't really believe her at the time. She said, "Do you have a ride to pick you up?"

I said, "Yes, my mom will be here." I called my mom ecstatic I could leave, and maybe I would be all right after this. They wheeled me out in a wheel chair with my belongings. I saw my mom outside and as they wheeled me through the open door, I felt the warm breeze hit my face. Fresh air I haven't experienced in days and really thought I would never feel again. I told my mom to wear two masks including a N95 one. The nurse helped me out of the chair into the car. It almost felt weird to leave as I was scared. Would I be all right without them? We pulled up to my home and I walked slowly inside and straight into the bedroom. The idea was to close the door and quarantine myself for ten days, doctors' orders. My mom would provide me food at the door and would have no contact. This time I will never forget how much I really needed her. I think sometimes we take for granted our loved ones. If she wasn't there I don't know if I could have taken care of myself. I will forever see how much my mom really loved me and wanted me to feel better and be Covid free. I crawled into my bed and felt at peace and that I was at once home. I looked around the room and saw my familiar pictures on the wall and there was my black cat waiting for me, and she never left my side that day. It's like she knew I was gone and may have never come back to the house. Just feeling the warmth of the bed, and my cat's presence next to me made me feel like I was whole again. Like I would outlive this and I would once again have a life. I do have to say I enjoyed every second of having food left for me and boy did I eat everything that was left for me. I never realized how much I loved Jello to be honest. Or pudding for that matter! These weird things I never liked before came to me as favorites. Almost unreal when I think back. I spent days in that bedroom, but I have to say I enjoyed every second of those walls that surrounded me. They were familiar and they were home. I watched endless television of random series and couldn't wait to get back to work. I loved to work, it made me feel alive and gave me a purpose in life. Even though that purpose seemed to dissipate as time went on, but when I laid there all I wanted was to get back to what made me smile and what made me wake up in the morning.

The News

I decided one of those long days in bed that I needed to share my story. I guess I was one of those crazy people that decided my awesome story of beating Covid had to be heard. People have asked me after if I still would have done it. The truth, hell yes! Nobody thought it could affect a healthy forty-year-old, the way it did me. Like I had to share this right? I mean, if not me, someone else I hope. The problem with sharing my story is people started picking it apart. I mean that is what humans do, right? They need to have someone to blame. The thing I found interesting in all of this is some blamed me and nothing happened to them. They didn't end up with Covid but boy did they have an opinion. So did some of their relatives for that matter. So, as I lay in my room finally just so happy that I am home, I get a call from one of the girls that was there over that weekend. Her conversation was short, thank goodness as I couldn't really deal with her as I was tired and almost lost my life. Overall, her conversation was something I won't ever forget. Let's call her Bulldozer as that is what it felt like when she called. Like I got hit by the biggest bulldozer of my life. So, she started asking me questions which was okay, fair enough. But her questions started to insinuate that I knew I had symptoms and shouldn't have gone. I thought all right, really, I just get out of hell and you Ms Bulldozer didn't even get this and you want to go into this right now. All right I guess, but wow is what I thought. I told Ms Bulldozer I can't believe you would bring this up right now as I am trying to get better and don't really feel the need to talk to you any further. We hung up and never really talked again. Which to me was a blessing because the next day I received this awesome message from her mom, saying that she wished me to have long lasting effects of the virus and that I put her daughter in harm's way. I can't explain the horror I felt reading the words. My heart hurt like it never had before. I mean, yes, I have had hurtful things said, I had relationships end in my life, but never in this format. Never someone wishing harm on me. I guess to this day it destroys my vision of life and human nature as a whole. All I could summon to write back was, "You should be ashamed of yourself. No one realizes they have this and gives this to someone on purpose." I got a virus and then felt like I was told I should have known I got it. If you look at this like an STD, no one was taking a precaution, we all went and we all took a risk with no protection. People could say this was risky behavior? You know maybe it was, but I wanted to live my life. I didn't want to be scared and I knew eventually I would get this virus. It spreads like the flu! You don't have to agree with me. I know some people stayed at home and never left those four walls, but at the time I just wanted to live life. I paid for that decision almost with my life. I got harassed about how I got the virus. It never mattered to me because I got it and I dealt with the repercussions of it. I lost friendships over it, I had individuals treat me differently afterwards. Guess everyone had their own opinion on how people were supposed to be or how they should react in a situation. Well guess what, we are all different on how we think and how we react. I never meant to put anyone in harm's way and I guess people can view it the way they want to. As more and more people get it maybe things will be different on the blame game, but during this time I was one of the early ones and people pointed fingers and made me feel terrible for contracting this. I guess that is why I am writing this now, as I don't know exactly why I am still here on this planet. I should have died, as I sure felt like that was the path I was on. I wonder to this day, if I had would all those people that made me feel terrible, would they still have showed up at the funeral? Would they have felt so bad that I perished to this awful virus? I guess I am glad I survived to know the true people in my life. The ones that wouldn't let a virus no one had real control of come between them. Now, we all have to wear masks and that is supposed to make it better as more and more get sick. Interesting, is all I have to say. The people that I thought were my friends, weren't, and that is so sad to be honest. I don't need sympathy because they know who they are and maybe they didn't really know me. Or maybe they did, but needed an excuse to exit the picture.

Which is all right looking back as no one needs fake people in their world. I asked myself, would I have acted like any of them? Oh, wait I got it, and possibly know where I got it from and I didn't, so I guess I answered my own question. As things got worse and yes, they did, our president even got it and they kept closing things down as the hospital beds got overwhelmed. I get it, I was one of those people in one of those beds. There are also a lot of people who got very little symptoms. This may be why I stayed alive to share this exact story and my thoughts on the matter. I think people should care, but not live-in fear. I never did and people can say that is why I ended up with it. The weird thing is that, if I died of this it would be all right because it in fact would have been my time. I knew that as I laid in that hospital bed that it may be my last breath. I wouldn't have blamed anyone, not even myself. It would have been the destiny that I was to walk through. I'm sure some people reading this are saying, you terrible human being. It's a virus people! When you go to your grocery store you put yourself at risk and everyone else. So much doesn't make sense about it, like we can eat outside in a tent but not inside a regular restaurant. I know we have to save lives, but what does this entail destroy, our economy? Destroy our social dynamics and those crucial hugs we all so long for. I still haven't hugged my mom! I miss her embrace and she is getting older, but am I ever going to hug her again? What if she dies tomorrow of something else? I will forever regret not giving her an embrace and a kiss on the cheek. Do I want to kill her with this? No, but the ever-ending loss of touch takes a toll on us. Well at least it has me through this whole thing. I lost friends along the way from this and to be honest I guess they weren't really my people, or my tribe you would say. I got a sickness and made it through and if they wanted to stop the journey with me then that was on them. I have always tried my best to believe the good and the best in people. This would sometimes make me fail in certain situations but I always knew deep down that I stood firm and was a person that cared about people. Sometimes people see certain things differently and at times make assumptions. I have myself done the same thing. I am still here and I have something to say. Life isn't what we all think it is. It's not about money or status. Some people are friends, but others wear masks and truly aren't your friends. Sometimes everything we think is real isn't. Sometimes there is a virus out there but the fear is worse than the virus itself. Wow, I guess that was what I wrote all this for, to say that it was real. I never had fear and still got it and almost died. Maybe this should be the end of the book, but wait I still have more.

Chapter 8

As I regained my strength and got back to where I was, it was a process. Friends that I thought were friends, weren't, and what I thought was my life suddenly became something I will never be able to explain. It's like you don't even know who you are any more, but deep down inside there is this light and you know it's there. People started to say hurtful things on social media that I would never have said to a single soul on this planet. They wished me harm and said, "I was a Covid Spreader." I would try and not engage in the comments, but you know how hard that is to not? How insulted and how angry a person can be when they just fought to stay alive? There are times now I wish I would have not fought so hard as this world is cruel. I still don't know why I was blessed to stay here there must have been something? Maybe I was supposed to share my story as it was the worst experience of my life. It's weird, as this is the part of the story I thought would flow and for some reason I am having a hard time with it. All I can think is that because I never really understood this part of humanity.

I had one person say, "They hoped I had further complications because I exposed someone they loved." I put this in quotations because those exact words were sent to me. That to me is not a nice human being and they really should be ashamed of themselves. Like I said, originally no one in their right mind wants to hurt anyone else. I mean, unless they are some kind of serial killer. Those words were like ice to me and I will not put a name to this person as they shouldn't be recognized for their undeniable ignorance. Nameless was best for them as no one should ever say something so insulting when there is a worldwide pandemic and they really should look at themselves. I hope they never go to the grocery store and hope they don't contract it from anywhere or they will for sure try to sue the very establishment. I learned a lot about people. How people's beliefs are presented and then demanded on to others. Not everyone is going to agree with everything, but it's how we present things and move forward in our lives. I seriously would never have treated someone so harshly. That is me though and others obviously have their own opinion on how to treat others. I think this is why this part is so hard because I have some very intense opinions on how people acted and how wrong it really was. It probably wouldn't matter because again, we all have our own opinion. But what was wrong is the harshness and the pointing of fingers. It was like the old witch hunt years ago. Own your own shit! I can I got Covid, may have exposed people to it which I am sorry, but in reality, I tried my best to do what I thought was right when I realized I was very sick. That is all that you can do. All the others I feel sorry for you, as most likely sorry to say people are going to get this and some will not make it or perish. This comes down to simple science and I almost died and can say it was all right. I got it and it made me a stronger person. I want to stand up to these people that were mean and they shouldn't have been. I want to scream at the top of my lungs, say I survived and that I hope so many others can say the same thing. I wish I could though trade places with someone that had so many more things to live for than I. I am a simple person, crazy man left and there is no plan just me. I wish I could trade myself to someone that had so much more to live for. That is what I wish! I mean I lost everything, the job I loved, the crazy man I adored and all the friends I thought were my friends. I will never understand the intentions above and maybe I was just meant to write this. That is seriously all I can think of now. I want others to be happy and realize that I almost lost my life and I don't know exactly know what to say, but remember every day is a blessing. Be kind to people, no one is perfect. Don't live in fear because that will destroy you more than anything. We are here to live to feel and to embrace other humans. The scariest thing of this whole pandemic was the actual fear it put into so many. People forgot what it meant to be human and started being distant and in lots of ways started to play the blame game. The fact is that the fear compromised us as a society, worse than the virus itself. It took away so many things and still to this day even as the virus is subsiding, has destroyed us as a group. There is no group any more, we were told to be inside away from others, that others were scary. So everyone that reacted to me in a negative way I say was caused undoability by fear. When I look back in history, the AIDS pandemic was very much the same way. People didn't want to touch you if they knew you had it. People were scared and made some feel unwanted and almost ostracized. This exact thing has occurred with Covid, a fear-based virus. I now know to this day so many good friends that have AIDS and as I move forward in my life, will know lots of people who have contracted Covid-19. I will never look down or criticize anyone that has contracted a virus. You can say well they were unsafe. Well, what does that exactly mean? Unsafe to you? We all have different opinions and that is what makes life so awesome. If you want to wear a mask, wear one. If you don't want to, don't make a big fuss to someone that doesn't hold the same view.

Chapter 9

Don't give up even when things feel like they are so imperfect and not all right. There may be something very important you need to accomplish first. I keep asking myself, why is this? What do I really want to say if this was my last thoughts? If you think about this it means something, and in reality, everyone would say something different. We all have something that would change our thoughts or our words. If there was something I could say, it would be that I thought life and certain people in my path were real and when confronted with a problem or something difficult, they ran away or were nowhere to be found. I will never truly understand this and I guess that is all right, maybe I am not supposed to totally get it? I think this is why I can't write any more, because in reality what does my opinion really matter? Does anyone really care I exist on this planet? Would all those people that made me feel terrible for contracting Covid come to my funeral? I mean let's be real, I hope they would never step foot there as they weren't really my people and wouldn't belong. If they did, I hope my real friends and people I adore would show them the door. Oh boy, here I am being an asshole again. I don't want fake people in my world any more. People that have a sort of an agenda or that if you don't meet will somehow make you feel less then or talk about you to others. I don't really know why I am still here, but I guess I am supposed to write something and tell you I fought for crazy man. When I didn't think anything could save me, I thought of him and that very life I wanted and dreamed of. I guess you can't always count your chickens till they hatch. At least that is what my grandma used to say. I guess he was here for that exact reason, to make me fight and to want to live. Maybe we aren't supposed to be with that exact person that we fought so hard for. But I will forever thank that person for coming into my life at that exact time in my life. If he didn't, I know in my heart I wouldn't have fought as hard as I did and I guess for whatever reason fate made me fight. So, here I am and I am confused and don't really know what I am doing here at times. I question this every day. My job has gone and I have a new one, but the passion is gone and I don't get the same feeling any more. I don't know who to trust now and I find myself just wanting to be alone. The passion though has to come from within you and that is what I have learned after this whole experience. It is all how you see it! Before I had Covid-19 I wasn't exactly happy with everything. I had these feelings of hopelessness. When I look back, I should have looked at things a little differently. I had everything most people would dream of.

This is the exact part that I had trouble with and I don't know exactly why. Maybe I had one of those stupid writer's block things people talk about. Or, maybe I just had to finish the exact chapter that this was in my life to really finish the explanation. Who knows really, but all I know is I am writing again, after months trying to finish what I have been trying to say. We all live here for a very short time and the reality is to make the very best out of every moment we get because tomorrow is not promised.

The weird thing is I thought I wanted to express all the negative things people said or expressed to me, but the reality is that it was all those things made me stronger and allowed me to be able to finish this the way it should be. None of those people meant any harm, they were just scared of the unknown which is what we as humans experience when we can't rationalize certain things. In reality the whole purpose of this is to say I am alive! I am in a totally different place then I would have ever thought a year after Covid. I am more on fire as a human then I have ever been. I found passion back in my life and embrace every change that crosses my path. So, Covid taught me to embrace change to not be scared any more about a single thing. It showed me that we are just here for a short amount of time and you have to make the utter best of it, or then you really lose. It's not the virus that makes you lose, it's actually us who don't see every day as a blessing and to encompass everything that comes across our paths in life. A pandemic, as this shows so many aspects of us, but all the others around us as well. I would have never done a thing different; I believe in living life. Even if I were to have died then in that fact it was part of living. I would never have changed a single thing. People can say I am selfish for feeling that way, I should have been more careful but in reality, life isn't about being careful. It is about living your life day to day and there is a risk in that. People will disagree with your choices but that is what makes us all different.

I am not with crazy man anymore and I loved him

dearly, but the paths in fact didn't meet up. He was there for his time to help me fight for my life and like I said I will always be grateful. I have learned I can't control everything and sometimes life actually leads you to somewhere beautiful not exactly where you expected but completely at peace. I'm not going to lie, I am still scared shitless, but not as much as I was before Covid-19. I found strength in people's negative words and judgements. I have found that I have to believe in positive things and they will happen as I am alive. I am here to tell my story and I guess it was a different ending then I expected. I didn't end up with the fairy tale I thought I would have. I ended up somewhere different and maybe the fairytale still exists, but it's not what I originally thought. I guess that's why I couldn't finish this until the actual Covid-19 chapter was complete and done. It was a year of my life I will never forget. People were mean but they were also kind to me. There was no control and nothing I can do to change a thing. I ended up exactly where I was supposed to be and I will forever be happy I embarked on this journey to write it. I always thought it would be amazing to have something written that would mean something to others. Like a little mark on this planet earth. I never thought it would be the Covid Girl, but I was and I will now embark on this new blessing of a journey and know there was a reason for me to stay alive. I have more things to do or else I wouldn't be here. I was supposed to live! I was supposed to conquer peoples' negativity and hurtful words. I survived for a reason and I will make every minute worth the extra time! I promise that!